GW00771273

SCENTING

ON THE

WIND

SCENTING
ON THE
WIND

Scentwork for Hunting Dogs

Susan Bulanda

Published by Doral Publishing, Sun City, Arizona
Printed in the United States of America.

Edited by Gwen Henson
Interior Design by The Printed Page
Cover Design by 1106 Design
Cover photo: Karin Ashe

Library of Congress Card Number: 2002103423
ISBN: 0-944875-52-1

Contents

Introduction

It was one of those great days to be out hunting with your dog. The sun was warm, the sky a cloudless deep blue. The air was filled with the wonderful smells of autumn: drying leaves and grasses and leaves burning in the distance. If you took a really deep breath, you could just catch the scent of apples in the air. For an autumn day, it was unusually dry and warm. The air was still, and it seemed quiet in the field.

My friend Lynn and I decided to take his Brittany spaniel, Corky, bird hunting. We were looking forward to a great day. As we pulled up to the game lands, I noticed that a few cars were parked in the parking lot, which meant other hunters were out trying their luck, too. Lynn, a guy who had hunted Brittanys for years, once told me that you could always tell the hunters who rode with Brittany spaniels in their car; they rode with their windows down, in all weather. After riding with Corky, I understood why. Corky was famous (and according to Lynn so are all Brittanys) for passing aromatic hydrocarbon's when excited. Lynn had a few good belly laughs as I groaned. I had to admit that I wanted to ride with my head out the window.

When we arrived, Corky jumped out of the truck and was ready to go. As soon as I had my gear on, we headed into the field. On command, Corky started to quarter, searching for the scent of birds. He was working hard, giving it his all. Corky was a good dog who had many successful hunts under his belt. Today he was turning up nothing. I knew that there were birds in the area because I had seen them. As we walked, I could hear the brush and grasses snap under my feet. It was the unmistakable sound of dried vegetation being crushed.

I could not understand why Corky could not find one measly little bird, or better yet, a nice fat one. Finally he came back to Lynn and looked at him as if to ask, "Are you sure there is something in this field?"

After a few hours, we headed back to the truck. On the way, a gentle breeze started moving the grasses and weeds. The breeze was blowing into our faces. The weather was also changing; it was getting cloudy and humid. It looked like it was going to rain later that night; you could smell the rain in the air. I also detected the smells of decay: mushrooms, rich undergrowth, and meadow grasses. I was sure that I smelled apples, even though I knew the closest apple orchard was three miles away—Whitney's orchard off Route 82. It was ridiculous. There was no way *my* sense of smell could catch apples from that far away. Then it occurred to me, if I could smell all of the different smells in the field, imagine what the dog could smell. On top of that, the dog had to sort it all out. A dog had to find the weaker scent of a pheasant or a grouse, birds that I couldn't imagine left all that much scent to begin with. Not like rabbits, whom I knew left quite a bit of scent behind—some friends had rabbits, and their hutches simply reeked. Turning into the wind, I took a deep breath and filled my head with all the smells the rich autumn day had to offer.

A thump on my leg brought me back to the task at hand. Corky was standing next to Lynn, looking up as if to say, "Let's try again."

I said to Lynn, "What, is that dog nuts?" Turning to Corky, I added, "We've been through this field once, and you couldn't find your tail with your nose if you tried." Corky gave me that happy dog look and just wagged his tail. "Oh, well," Lynn said, "Let's give it a try." We started Corky into the wind. Within ten minutes, he found a bird, a beautiful bird that would grace the table for Sunday dinner. When we returned to the parking lot, we met some of the other hunters. Some had no luck at all and some had similar experiences to our own—no success in the early afternoon but some luck later.

I gave Corky a slap on the side for a good job, got into the truck, rolled the windows down, and said to Lynn and Corky, "Let's go home." Although it wasn't a bad day, that day years ago—more years than I care to remember—was typical of dozens of others. I noticed that on certain days the dogs did better than on others. What was the difference? Before I worked with Lynn and Corky, I had worked a beagle and a Springer spaniel. I had noticed the same pattern. The pattern was too consistent to write it off as the dog having a bad day or a good day.

Finally, I noticed that the weather and wind were the consistent elements that dictated the way my dogs worked. This observation started my research into the effects of wind and weather on scent work. It was during this time that I developed my first concepts about scent work. Being very young, I was sidetracked by life and never pursued the sport of hunting. I went on to obedience training, sled dog racing, and search and rescue work. However, the experience of working with a hound and a bird dog impressed me very much. Later, I became involved in human tracking with dogs. The more I got involved with scent work, I realized that no matter what you are looking for, certain aspects of scent work are the same. While the object of the search is different and the scent is different, THE WAY THE DOG FINDS THE SCENT is the same.

This book will outline scenting conditions, weather conditions, and grid patterns. When these elements are applied to the hunting dog, it will give the hunter the edge over those who do not consider these elements. Although most of my experience is in search and rescue, the strategies for finding scent apply to hunting.

This book is not a step-by-step training guide for hunting dogs. There are many trainers who are better at training hunting dogs

Golden Retriever pups in training on a cold winter day.
Photo courtesy of Sue VanBuren

than I am. This book does explain how to set up training problems to use the weather and wind so that scent is available to the dog. It is my goal to explain how to give your dog the experience he or she needs to learn to use the wind to find the scent of game. However, the dog is half of the team. The dog's human partner is the other half. The hunter must understand grid techniques to direct his or her dog into the best situations to use the wind and weather. These techniques have been proven and used throughout the world by search and rescue dog handlers to find missing people. These strategies will help both the people who hunt in the field and the people who want to compete in field trials.

The strategies that I have outlined in this book are taken from my book *READY! The Training of the Search and Rescue Dog. READY!* was the first detailed book of its kind on the subject. In 1994, *READY!* was nominated as best book by the Dog Writers Association of

America. In 1996, it won first place in its class in the National League of American Pen Women's award. *READY!* has been translated into a number of languages and adopted worldwide. Around that time, Mr. Stephen L. Duren, a columnist for *The Maine Sportsman*, reviewed a copy of *READY!*. Mr. Duren liked the sections on scent work so much that he recommended it to sportsmen. Because of his review, I realized that the principles of *READY!* could be put into a book for sportsmen and their dogs. So this book owes its existence to Mr. Stephen L. Duren.

Maggie, 10-month-old. WC
Tonawanda Wildlife Refuge, Wolcottsville, NY

1

Choosing the Dog and Socialization

The Dog

The first step is to find the right dog. If you do not have a dog, you need to decide which breed you want and then find a good breeder. Check with your local breed club, hunt club, or one of the dog registries. The registry that many hunting dog breeders use is the United Kennel Club (UKC). The other registry, which deals more with show dogs, is the American Kennel Club (AKC). You can find both on the Internet or in hunting magazines. Once you locate a few breeders, you need to select which one has the dogs that you like. To start with, go and see their dogs. Be sure to ask for a demonstration of the sire and dam in the field. After all, that is your main goal for getting a dog. Keep in mind that you must try to determine how much of the dog's ability is instinct and how much is training. The next step is to ask for the names of the puppies that the breeder has sold from the parents you like. Call the owners, and ask them to tell you about their dogs.

Here is a handy checklist to help you decide if the breeder is the kind of person with whom you want to work.

An ethical breeder will:

- Stand behind his or her dogs
- Answer your questions
- Breed only one or two litters a year
- Not breed a bitch on consecutive heats
- Breed only one or two breeds of dog
- Have clean facilities
- Have healthy dogs
- Not push breeding contracts
- Let you bring any and all contracts to your lawyer
- Have a solid socialization program for his or her puppies
- Have proven the sire and dam's working ability

Once you are ready to select a puppy, there are a few simple rules to help you make the selection. First, do not pick a puppy based on color or sex. The puppy's instinct, intelligence, and temperament are your first concern. When you initially go to see the litter at about eight weeks of age, go alone. Do not bring the family. At least have them wait in another room so you can evaluate the puppies alone for a few minutes. When you first enter the room alone (without the breeder) take note of which puppy runs to you first. Then walk around the room and see which puppy follows you the longest. You do NOT want the pup that ran to you first, nor do you want the pup who stays back and does not come over to you. Ideally, you want the pup who follows you the longest. This is most likely going to be the most people-motivated pup in the litter. The pup that ran to you first is the most dominant pup and most likely was trying to bully the other pups. This is a potential problem dog. The dog that stays with you is the one who is most people oriented and has the ability to focus the longest.

Ashley (Flat-coat Retriever) and Golden Retrievers, Stoney, Telcey, and Maggie
Photo courtesy of Sue VanBuren

If you already have a dog, the only way to find out if he or she will hunt is to try him or her. Some dogs that you think will not work can fool you and turn out to be the best hunting dogs. Others will seem to be a prime candidate and then turn out to be unmotivated or unsuitable for hunting. While it is true you can train any dog to do anything given the correct method and motivation, I feel that if a dog does not show a genuine interest in the work early in training, this may be an indication that the dog lacks an acceptable level of instinct to hunt. In order to do a good job in adverse situations, the dog must love the work. The dog must have a strong drive to find game.

Although you may prefer one breed to another, it all comes down to the individual dog. The ideal hunting dog is calm, bold, and confident, not aggressive or overly dominant. He or she should also be people motivated. In other words, a dog who bonds with his or her owner properly is usually eager and willing to please and is easier to train. While the bonding to humans has nothing to do with the dog's hunting ability, it has everything to do with the control that you have over your dog. This is what makes a dog biddable or willing to take commands from you. Another characteristic to look for is a dog that demonstrates a preference for using his or her nose rather then finding game with his or her eyes. The dog should be curious in new situations or of new objects. He or she will have the physical size and build to handle all types of obstacles in the environment that you will be hunting. He or she should be young and healthy enough to give you years of work. Keep in mind that many working dogs start to lose their stamina at around eight to nine years of age.

One of the most important considerations is that the dog not have any genetic defects. Those dogs bred solely for conformation show purposes should be cautiously evaluated since they may not have the instinct and intelligence required for the demands of field work.

Socialization

One of the first requirements of a hunting dog is that he or she be confident and social. Aggression toward man or animals is absolutely unacceptable. The dog must be able to work well in excitable, high stress situations. The dog must be able to handle all types of noise and unusual physical conditions. This is important if you hunt in areas of the country where suburban sprawl has cut into your hunting areas or if you plan to compete in field trials. Keep in mind that your dog can hear what is going on farther away than you can. The best way to insure that your dog will handle these types of situations is to socialize him or her. The younger you start your dog, the more easily he or she will become socialized. The ideal age to start is seven or eight weeks. Generally, until the dog has had proper shots and is nine to ten weeks of age, primary socialization should take place in the home.

Socializing your dog is not difficult, but it is time consuming. It requires more than just taking your dog with you wherever you go. You must plan ahead in order to be able to introduce your dog to different situations. Depending upon where you live, this could involve an all day outing. When you plan your socialization excursions, keep in mind that in many situations you will want to have adequate control over your dog, which will require some obedience work. You should start puppy training at home a few days after you get your pup, or right away if you get an older dog. The training process is a form of socialization and helps to develop a bond between you and the dog. It also helps if, when you take your dog into the field, he or she will come when called. It is important for you to walk your dog in both city and country settings. The dog must get used to and accept all types of strangers petting him or her, must allow children to hug him or her around the neck and kiss him or her on the face. This is an ideal way to prevent future lawsuits, which could result if your dog is not friendly to people.

Socialization should focus on the smells and sounds of the city. This should include the noise generated by construction work, including heavy equipment, jackhammers, etc. Heavy construction work will cause vibrations through the ground as well as loud noise. The dog should experience the smell of different fuels (from a distance) such as are generated by diesel equipment as well as gas, propane, and electric equipment. It is also a good idea to get the dog used to different types of footing and flooring. The dog should be able to walk on different ground and floor surfaces to include, but not be limited to, slick, rough, uneven, and moving surfaces (such as an elevator). The dog should also be exposed to the sights and smells of the country, including farm equipment. The dog should not be frightened by nor want to chase livestock and household pets. If you live in an area that has cliffs and mines, the dog can be introduced to and

Timberline Bassett Hound Club Hunting Test
Photo courtesy of Carol Makowski

taught to be wary of these dangers. This is especially important since a dog's sense of distance and depth perception are not as good as humans'. He or she should be able to swim in lakes and ponds, cross streams, and navigate logs, boulders, ravines, gullies, and hills. The dog should experience walking through and near the various types of vegetation that he or she will encounter. The dog should experience the feel and sound of strong wind and weather in both country and city environments.

Part of his or her socialization should include trips to both a small and a large airport. If possible, the dog should be flown in small aircraft and helicopters. If flying is not possible, he or she should be loaded into and out of aircraft while the motor is both off and running. The dog should also be introduced to boats—both around and in them.

Socialization should include going to nursing homes and visiting people who move slowly and use special equipment to get around. The sight of a person in a wheelchair or who uses crutches can be upsetting to a dog that has never seen this before. Be inventive, use your imagination, and introduce your dog to everything you can think of. For the situations that your dog has not experienced, his trust and confidence in you as well as himself, will give him what he needs to handle whatever comes his way.

The most important thing about socialization is to be sensible. You do not want to introduce your dog or puppy to situations in a manner that will frighten him or her since this will defeat the purpose of socialization. The hidden benefit of socializing your dog the way I have described is that when he or she is not hunting, your dog could be a candidate for therapy dog work or other similar types of activities. This is a wonderful thing for any children in the home to do with your dog. It will also give your dog a rewarding life beyond the field.

Initial shyness or insecurity in a puppy is nothing to be too concerned about since it is usually an indication that the pup just needs some socialization. Many puppies go through a period of shyness, which they overcome with proper handling. However, if the dog is a year or more in age, shyness and fear warrant a little more concern. The older the dog, the more serious the problem. If the older dog does not adjust to strangers within a few training sessions, coupled with a concentrated socialization effort on the part of the owner, the dog's suitability for hunting should be seriously evaluated by a competent dog trainer or canine behaviorist.

There are many trainers and dog people who are hung up on the dominance, alpha concept concerning their dogs. Some claim it is not a desirable practice to allow puppies to mouth people. They feel that all interaction between dog and owner should be with owner dominance in mind. This viewpoint eliminates some of the interaction between dog and owner that usually takes place in the form of play. Some go so far as to say it is not acceptable to allow the dog to stand over you, stare at you, to hug the dog, etc. On the contrary, it is important for a young puppy to be allowed to use his or her mouth to play with humans as well as other animals. It is important to teach the dog to develop bite inhibition, or learn to control his or her mouth. It is also very important for the potential hunting dog to learn to relate to people in all kinds of personal situations. The dog that is forbidden to stand over a human, with the human in a prone position, may not know how to relate to such an experience.

It is important for the dog to learn to play with his or her owner, as well as other people. All types of interaction with the dog will give your dog the ability to understand the difference between play and work. During training or work, the dog must be obedient, and play must take place in a controlled manner. This teaches the dog to be controlled when he or she is excitable and also builds trust and confidence in the dog. During play, it is okay to let the dog win and play at being alpha with you, as long as the play ends with you in control over the dog. The best way to establish your alpha position is to run through the obedience commands quickly and give the dog hearty praise for obeying the commands. What confuses the dog the most are mixed messages. An example of a mixed message to a dog would be the dog who does something the owner does not want, the owner says "no" to the dog, usually in a rather meek tone of voice, and pats the dog, thinking the pat is a gentle slap. In reality, the dog understood the pat as praise for the behavior. Dogs do not understand English, and when the tone of voice is meek, the dog can interpret the owner's reaction as praise for the behavior that the owner does not want.

Play interaction with your dog is an important part of socialization. The dog should be encouraged to play with many different people of all sizes, races, and ages. The dog should learn how to roll around with people, play in an excitable manner, have people (usually children) crawl under him and over him, have people reach over him, touch him, and so on. In essence, do what you want to do. Show affection by holding his or her head and gazing into his or her eyes while whispering sweet nothings. It is an important part of the dog/human bond.

2

Concepts of Dog Training and Philosophies

To best use the material in this book, you should know what type of hunting you want to teach your dog and the training techniques you want to employ. Another very important aspect of training a dog is your idea about the dog's mind and how it works. This should be clear to you before you start training your dog. You may not think that your view of your dog's mind is important, but it is. If you do not feel that a dog thinks, you will use one type of training technique. If you feel that your dog has very limited mental abilities, you may use another type of training. If you feel that your dog is very intelligent, it opens your mind to a new set of techniques.

Your philosophy about dogs will also flavor how you interpret why your dog does what it does. Keep in mind that no one will ever truly know how dogs think and what they feel. Only the dogs and God know that. Nor will anyone ever know exactly how intelligent dogs are. However, as scientists develop new tests, we gain more insight into what goes on in a dog's mind. Different training methods and

TLC Jackpot Kid Maggie, a 7-month-old Golden Retriever swims back with her prize.
                    Photo courtesy of Sue VanBuren

tests suggest that dogs are more intelligent than once was thought. Observations and studies have opened the door to new theories about the emotions of animals. It is a good idea to evaluate just what you feel about the intelligence and emotions of dogs.

By the way, new research suggests that dogs do see color. I think this is important for a dog handler to know. When dogs hunt, they not only use their sense of smell, but they use their hearing and sight as well. Dog handlers tend to forget this and focus only on the sense of smell.

The Job At Hand

Before you set up a training problem for your dog, be sure that *YOU* understand exactly what must take place for the dog to learn. Review the details of the task, and break it down into the smallest steps possible. Remember, initially the dog is working on his or her instinct. That instinct may drive him to find game, but it will not tell the dog how you want him to do it. Nor will your dog's instincts tell him which game to find. At least his instincts will not tell him which game to *ignore*. It is your responsibility to teach the dog how to work with you and not just run around aimlessly chasing all game.

Dogs Do Not Speak English

This is probably the most important concept to keep in mind. Not only do dogs not speak English, but as far as we can tell, their system of communication is not based on verbalizations. Therefore, it would be reasonable to assume that they do not even THINK in verbal terms. What is important to a dog is your body language. This includes your facial expressions and the tone of your voice. Because our body language and tone of voice reflect our ATTITUDE, it is important to have a *positive* attitude while training a dog. If you do not believe your dog will do the work, you hinder the dog's ability to learn. This is because your negative attitude will show through in your whole body. If you are having a bad day or do not feel well, do not work your dog. If you try to work your dog when you feel this way, you typically will find that you cannot hide it from your dog.

Use A Whistle

An excellent way to signal to a dog in the field is to use a whistle. Remember, dogs do not speak English. The sound of a whistle can travel farther than a human's voice. The dog can also hear the whistle easier when there are other noises such as wind, water, or road noise. Whistles do not show emotions. Lastly, the whistle saves the hunter's voice. An excellent whistle to use is a sheep-herding whistle. Designed to be heard by the dog as far as one mile away, it allows you to make an endless variety of sounds. See Appendix I for suppliers.

Proper Tone of Voice

When you are in a situation where you will voice command your dog, remember that the tone of your voice is as important as your body language. Together they make up the primary means that you use to communicate with your dog. You must make your tone of voice directional or no nonsense. You tone shouldn't be questioning, dictatorial, or hysterical, and it should not be loud. A dog has a very acute sense of hearing. Do not yell at your

Alya of White Water on a hunting trip, Eastern Oregon
Photo courtesy of Joan Bailey

Bailey of Ocean House in Maine
Photo by Rick Moh

dog; keep the volume of your voice between soft and normal. When the dog does what you want, you should raise the *tone* of your voice to praise the dog, not the volume. When you correct the dog, lower the tone to suit the correction. The most severe correction should be a growling sound. If you speak to your dog within her range of hearing and she does not respond, she may just be ignoring you!

Negative Reinforcement

Negative reinforcement is different from punishment. Negative reinforcement is something that is not pleasant and which can be stopped by ceasing the activity that is not acceptable. Auto manufacturers use negative reinforcement to get us to fasten our seat belts and close our doors. The annoying buzzer or bell that rings until we hook the seat belt is negative reinforcement. When you hook the belt, the sound stops. After awhile, you will hook the belt immediately to prevent the annoy-ing bell. Negative reinforcement has trained you to do what the auto manufacturer wishes you to do. An example of the use of negative reinforcement with dogs is the "Invisible Fence." The Invisible Fence gives the dog a warning if he or she comes too close to the boundary, fol-lowed by an electric shock for getting too near the boundary. If the dog wants to eliminate the shock, he or she has to move away from the boundary.

Punishment

Generally, you will find that avoiding both punishment and negative reinforcement tech-niques will produce the best hunting dog. Instead of punishing your dog, show your dog what you want him or her to do. Sometimes this will involve communicating to the dog that the behavior he or she has exhibited is not correct. To do this, you can lean forward, make eye contact, then in a deep growling voice, say "NO." When the dog stops the unwanted behavior, praise him. If you find you are correcting a dog more than you are praising the dog, it is time to reevaluate your training technique.

Punishment techniques are different from negative reinforcement techniques (see above). Punishment typically does not have lasting positive results. This is because punishment happens regardless of whether the activity stops or not. You get punished for what you did no matter what. Punishment is usually a coercive act a handler inflicts upon a dog as a reaction

*Alya of White Water during Utility Field Test for fully
trained versatile hunting dog*
                    Photo courtesy of Joan Bailey

to unwanted behavior. The coercive act usually causes some degree of pain or discomfort
to the dog. Examples of punishment are a
shock from a shock collar, painful sound, slaps,
punches, pinches, or leash jerks. Although
punishment sometimes gives short-term results,
it is not conducive to the dog's well being and it
may inhibit the dog's desire to please.

   Punishment is usually the reaction of a
frustrated dog owner. When you punish a dog
because of frustration, you are inclined to over-
correct or overpunish the dog. It is easy to give
in to the desire to punish more severely when
the lesser level of punishment doesn't give
immediate results. Some dogs that are over-
corrected to the point where they feel they are
put on the defensive, will bite. Punishing the
hunting dog can cause him or her to associate
the unpleasant experience with hunting. He or
she may not want to hunt again.

Teach and Show

The hunting dog's instincts will drive him or her to pursue game. However, the control he needs and the fine points of his techniques must be taught. Therefore, when you train a dog, remember he does not have a clue about how you want him to behave. You must structure your training in such a manner that you show the dog what you want him to do. Then be sure to reward him for doing it. It is very unfair to punish a dog for not doing what you want when he does not understand what is expected of him.

Commands

Whatever commands or whistle signals you decide to use, be sure to be consistent in your use of them. A command should always equal an action, either on your part or the dog's part. He or she either obeys, or you teach. Never stand and repeat a command to a dog. Remember, dogs do not speak English. If your

Alya of White Water
Photo courtesy of Joan Bailey

Remine, a Weimaraner
       Photo courtesy of Russell DiGiallorenzo

dog does not know what the word "sit" means and you tell your dog to "SIT, SIT, SIT," he or she will not know that S-I-T is one word. He or she will think SITSITSIT is the command. Then, depending upon how you react to this situation, the dog may learn not to sit until the third time you say "sit." By repeating commands, you also teach the dog it is OK to respond when he or she feels like doing so or that he or she does not have to respond at all. Rationalizing for your dog's lack of response to you only encourages the repetition of the response. This is because you allow the dog to disobey if he or she knows what the command means, or you allow your dog to obey in a way that is not suitable to you. In cases where the dog does not know what the command means, you teach him or her the wrong response. People who repeat commands often do not

Remine, a Weimaraner
       Photo courtesy of Russell DiGiallorenzo

realize that they assume that the dog either: 1) understands the command and just refuses to obey or, 2) does not hear the command. Frequently both assumptions are incorrect. You must define the manner in which you want your dog to respond to a command and stick to it.

Be Inventive

Even hunting dogs get bored with training. This is why it is important not to get into a rut of methods and styles. Different things work for different exercises. Not all methods work all of the time for all dogs. Do not hesitate to try different ways to communicate to your dog and to motivate your dog. Changing different aspects of training—even things like location, time, and day of week can help get a dog out of a rut.

Motivate

The key to successful dog training is to motivate your dog properly. A dog will never learn anything unless it is meaningful to him or her. Proper motivation makes the lesson meaningful to your dog. Again, different things motivate different dogs. Use whatever works. If your dog is motivated to work for food, then use food. If he or she likes to play, use play as a reward. Many dog trainers use punishment techniques to teach a dog. This method is especially undesirable for training the hunting dog. The dog must love the work and enjoy it. The dog who hunts only because he or she is afraid of being punished will not work consistently and reliably. Nor will he or she work as long. An excellent technique of dog training is the "click and treat" method. It requires dog handlers to be open minded and to change their training methods. This method of training provides great rewards because it encourages the

Remine, a Weimaraner
Photo courtesy of Russell DiGiallorenzo

dog to think and work. See the Appendix for where to get "click and treat" materials.

Food Reward

Many traditional dog trainers absolutely refuse to use a food reward in training. There are continuing debates about the use of food as motivation for a dog in training. When using food, be sure the focus of the reward is your reward signal (click, whistle, verbal praise, petting, etc.) and then the food. To do this, give your dog the signal and then the tiny morsel of food. The whole process should only take a few seconds. It does not matter what kind of food you use, however, it should be semimoist, which will allow you to regulate the correct size of the tidbit. The reward should never be larger then one-quarter inch square. It is intended as a tease, something the dog will work harder to get more of. The food must be very desirable to the dog. It should not be

Remine

Photo courtesy of Russell DiGiallorenzo

Russell DiGiallorenzon and Remine
Photo courtesy of Russell DiGiallorenzo

given every time and gradually should be withdrawn and substituted with praise. If you reward the dog for every act, the food reward will lose its motivation for the dog. As the dog succeeds at one level, he or she must work harder to get the treat.

Food training has some very interesting points to consider. First, a dog who is fearful or in pain will not respond to a food reward. This means if you use a food reward successfully, your dog is learning in a fearless and painless environment. This type of environment is very necessary for the hunting dog. Some trainers claim the dog will work for food and not out of love for the owner. However, if your bond with the dog is strong, your dog will work for you out of love. The food is just a pleasant addition and an added motivator. You do not have to starve a dog to use a food reward. We are not talking about making the dog work to earn his or her food in order to keep from starving. He or she is only earning the extra special treat. If the dog does not perform to the level you want, you do not withhold his or her dinner. (Please note, due to the risk of torsion and bloat, it is not a good idea to work a dog right after he or she eats his or her dinner. Check with your veterinarian to learn more about torsion and bloat.)

Food reward is a proven method commonly used in all levels of animal training. It is even used as a motivator for children. Earning the extra tidbit can increase the dog's inventiveness by allowing him or her to develop ways to earn his or her special treat. A study by Margaret Gibbs illustrated that dogs learn quicker and are more eager to work when the reward is food. The study illustrates that food works much better than the traditional punishment techniques or hand signals.

Further validity for food as a reward has been illustrated by researchers at the Veterans Administration Medical Center in Sepulveda, California. They have discovered that a dog's memory is enhanced by hormones released during feeding. The implication of the study is that if a dog is fed after training, it will enhance his or her memory, enabling the dog to better retain what he or she has learned. If food works, use it, but it must be used properly. Food is not meant to be a bribe for the dog, but a reward for proper behavior or performance.

(For two interesting articles on food reward, see the April 1990 issue of the *Pure-Bred Dogs/*

Am/Can Ch Blacfriar TLC Classic Ashley, WC,
a Flat-coat Retriever
Photo courtesy of Sue VanBuren

American Kennel Gazette, "Food For Thought" by Patricia Gail Burnham, pages 80-83 and "To Treat or Not To Treat" by Margaret Gibbs, pages 84-89.)

Food rewards can be used to shape the behavior of the hunting dog in order to "fine tune" his or her hunting techniques. For those who still feel that a dog will work for food and not love, consider this. You feed your dog his or her dinner every day and he or she still loves you!

Keep the Goal of Each Exercise In Mind

For some dogs, it is better to have training sessions that focus on the problem area. For example, if you want to teach the dog to hold his or her point longer, then do not mix that goal with other training exercises. Make the entire session for the day an exercise on holding the point.

TLC Jackpot Kid Maggie at 6 months
WNYRC Sanctioned Trial, 1st Place Junior Puppy
Photo courtesy of Sue VanBuren

Often people get sidetracked while train-ing a dog, or they try to teach the dog too much at once. Be sure to identify the goal of the exercise and work toward it.

If Your Dog Doesn't Get It

What should you do if your dog does not respond to your training exercise? Go back to the previous step and/or try different tech-niques or motivation methods. When your dog cannot seem to grasp what you are trying to teach him, it is usually because you have not clearly defined the rules of the particular exer-cise. You may have given the dog the option of choosing whether he or she wants to work or not. (See: If Your Dog Refuses To Work) In most cases, he or she probably doesn't under-stand what you want him or her to do. If this is the problem, reevaluate the exercise and break it into smaller steps. An example is the dog who will not stay for the long down. To correct this, start by downing the dog and waiting for a few seconds before praising him. Instead of increasing the length of the down by ten second segments, vary the time required to stay. Make him or her stay for five seconds, then fifteen. Next five and then ten, then ten, five, and fifteen. Do this until the dog can hold the stay for a length of time that is *longer* than you want. As he or she stays for you, increase the length of the down until you can walk around the corner of a building and the dog will stay. If you just walked away for twenty minutes without working up to it, the dog would never learn to stay.

If your dog cannot seem to grasp the exercise you are trying to teach him or her, it may be because the dog did not understand the previous step in the training. If your dog has problems at any level of training, go back to the previous level and be sure he or she knows it before you advance to the next level. When you first perform an exercise, sometimes the dog may seem to grasp it in the first training session. In reality, your dog will not have fixed the lesson in his or her long-term memory. By the next session, you may have to retrain the dog. This is especially true for younger or immature dogs. Young dogs have not had the experience and practice learning how to understand you that an older dog has had. The young hunting dog will need practice controlling his or her zeal to find game. He or she must learn that you are the other half of the team.

A dog should not move on to the next level until he or she can perform the previous level "in his or her sleep." The time this will take will vary from dog to dog and exercise to exercise. A fair guide is twenty to fifty repetitions over a period of time. Do not try to do it in a day or a week.

If Your Dog Refuses To Work

Sometimes you may feel your dog knows an exercise and refuses to do it. Many people feel this is stubbornness or defiance in a dog, when in reality it may be just a lack of response. There are several possibilities for this behavior. To begin with, he or she may not have learned the exercise thoroughly. You may think he or she knows the work, but in reality he or she does not. All dogs will learn at their own rate. There is nothing you can do to change this. Another possibility could be the dog does not feel well. You must always rule out a physical reason for a lack of response. You cannot

Ch. Kinnike Justin JH
Photo courtesy of John Bandes

expect a dog that is in pain from a prior muscle pull or injury to work for you.

Also, you must take a close look at your training techniques. Nothing will make a dog's desire to work diminish or break his or her confidence more than punishment. Examine your techniques if your dog refuses to work. Most people yell when they become angry. This in turn can cause a dog to become frightened. Punishment often follows, and that causes more fright and less response from the dog. It becomes self-perpetuating with no positive results. You cannot teach when you are angry because you are reacting to the situation instead of being in control. You must be in control to teach. If your dog makes a mistake, do not correct this mistake by punishing him. An improper response from your dog is not the end of the world. It will not ruin your dog or undo his or her training. Instead, go back and prompt him or her to do the correct thing, and reward him or her for doing it. Your sloppy handling of the exercise can cause the quality of your dog's performance to slip. You may have inadvertently taught the dog to perform at a different level than you intended. Therefore, when you do not get the level of performance you want, reevaluate yourself and the dog.

You must also consider the possibility of canine burnout. If you suspect this or you can't figure out why the dog refuses to work, try giving him or her a few weeks off. Remember, although it is fun for you and your dog, hunting is very stressful. This is especially true for the dog, whose level of excitement is usually higher than the human. Be sure to keep in mind that if you are stressed or suffering burn-out, the dog will react to your attitude.

Regression can be a problem in training. For various reasons, the dog will regress and seem to forget what he or she has learned. Usually this happens when training is stopped for too long. Also a dog can be inadvertently untrained or retrained so that the former work is undone. This can also happen if a dog is bored or unmotivated. In this situation, it is best to start over from the beginning and retrain the dog. Typically the retraining will take less time.

You must also consider the weather and the time of year. It is possible that the game or scent is not available. You may think your dog is not working when in reality he or she cannot find game. The ability to judge if your dog is working or not comes with learning how to read your dog. It also comes with practice.

Short Lessons

If you keep the lessons short, you will not bore or tire your dog. He or she will like the work much better. Once the dog has learned what he or she is supposed to do, you can work him or her for longer periods. It is especially important to keep the lessons very short when you are training a young dog. The younger a dog is, the shorter his or her attention span. Because young hunting dogs are very excited, they burn out more quickly. Watch your dog closely, and keep the lessons as short as is practical.

Ch. Kinnike Wesley SH
Photo courtesy of John Bandes

Age To Start

Dogs as young as eight weeks of age can start with the games that lead up to hunting. When your puppy is bonded to you, settled enough in its new home, and healthy, you can start training games. If you get your pup at eight weeks of age, you can start training at about ten to twelve weeks of age. If you get an older pup, give him or her a few weeks to settle in. When you start a very young puppy or dog, it is important to keep the work light and to give the dog time off. It is easy for the dog handler to get too intense too soon. This can cause burnout in a dog and/or handler. It is easy to forget how young a dog is when he or she grows physically so fast. Think of it, a six-month-old dog has only had four months of life experience. His or her first eight weeks or two months were spent with his or her litter. That is not much time for the dog to understand humans! Yet many dog owners expect

Ch Kinnike Siimon JH
Photo courtesy of John Bandes

that by six months of age, the dog's behavior will be well on the way to what they expect from an adult dog.

Start Exercise Signal

You should have some sort of signal to let the dog know 1) training or work is to begin and 2) which type of work is expected. If you plan to cross train your dog to do different types of work, the second point is an important aspect of training. Your dog can tell by your clue that he or she is to hunt as opposed to doing obedience work, etc. Some people use a special collar or harness to signal to the dog what is expected of him or her. It could also be a certain short routine, but should not be the actual command for the first exercise. For example, you can let your dog know training time has arrived by repeating a certain phrase, such as "Let's go train" before you begin the training. Do not use a training command such as "heel" as a signal that the training is to begin. The main function of the start exercise signal is to build up the dog's excitement or anticipation of what he or she is expected to do. Often with hunting, the sight and sound of you getting your gear together will do this, but do not depend on this as your signal. The signal can be a short routine such as slapping the dog's side and telling him or her to get ready for work. Whatever you decide to use, it must be consistent and used all of the time.

End Of Exercise Signal

This is similar to the Start Exercise Signal, except its purpose is to let the dog know he or she is finished. It is a release command or routine. Some people just give the dog the command "FINISHED" which lets the dog know he or she is free from the work. The Start Exercise and End Work Signal are most important to use during training sessions when it may be the least clear to the dog when the training sessions begin and end. Imagine that you are doing an obedience routine with your dog. You have just finished a "heel" exercise, and you look at your watch. You realize that you have to leave now to meet someone. So you simply turn and walk away. What is the dog supposed to do or think? The end exercise signal lets him or her know he or she is dismissed.

Ch Kinnike Jameson MH, Breed's First Champion Master Hunter, Owner: Kinnike Kennels and Cush Phillips

Photo courtesy of John Bandes

Wrong Response Signal

This is not a "NO" but a calm word used to let the dog know that the response he or she has given you is not the one you want. No punishment is given, but a reward is withheld instead. Use the "wrong response" signal along with the "correct response" signal. This way you can let the dog know what behavior is correct and what behavior is not the one you want.

Game Play Reward

For most hunting dogs, the drive to find game is strong enough that the activity itself is a reward. However, for those dogs whose drive is not that strong, this is probably the most important aspect of training a dog to hunt. Besides pleasing you, the reward game should elicit a high level of motivation for doing the work. After awhile, the dog will transfer the reward to finding the game. To make this transfer, he or she must have a fun activity to associate with finding the game.

Not all dogs are play motivated. Some individual dogs (and some breeds) are very serious. As mature adults, they do not want to play. Some people feel that all dogs can learn to play. They feel that those dogs who do not want to play are serious because they were not played with by their owners. They feel that this attitude results from an "all work and no play" attitude by the owner. Yet others feel that animals do not play for the fun of it at all. Animal play is the result of a behavior directed by instincts, which makes it a drive. One example is the need or drive of the retriever to fetch objects, often called a compulsive retriever. This is also visible in the Border collie as the drive or need to gather livestock and bring them to the handler. Although both breeds have a different purpose for the behavior, the results are the same. The dog will find the most satisfaction if the game involves an activity that allows him or her to do what he or she was bred to do. The problem lies in that many breeds no longer have the drive to do what they were bred to do.

Regardless of what you believe and how your dog may act, you can teach the dog to play. You can teach a dog to have a meaningful routine with you that the dog will look forward to and enjoy. All that is required is a dog that likes to be with you and do things with you. Thus, the motivating factor in developing the routine will be the dog's desire to interact with you. The success of the routine will depend upon how well the dog is bonded to you. When you are trying to invent a game for your dog, observe what he or she likes to do best, and capitalize on it by incorporating it into a game. Be sure, though, that the behavior is an acceptable behavior. A good game for the hunting breeds is letting the dog search through your pockets for a tidbit. The key is to be inventive. Be sure to develop the game prior to training to hunt. The hunt training sessions are not the time or place where you teach your dog his or her reward game.

Be Consistent

If you keep changing your personal techniques with your dog, he or she will never know what you want. When you train your dog, be consistent in your methods. This includes your methods of praise, corrective tone of voice, corrective technique, and the method you use to show the dog what you want. Also be sure to use the same commands for the behavior you want. You cannot do the recall with a "COME" once and "GET OVER HERE" the next time and expect your dog to understand what you want.

Senses

Most dog owners are aware that a dog has a keen sense of smell and hearing, but there are misconceptions about the other senses. We cannot be one hundred percent certain about a dog's vision. However, new research has shown that dogs see a full range of colors. Bear

*Dual Ch Kinnike Blackthorne pointing, Dual Ch/Am
Field Ch, Kinnike Wythelde backing*
                    Photo courtesy of John Bandes

in mind that the research is inconclusive, and
there is a possibility that dogs do not see every
shade of every color. For those who doubt that
a dog can see color at all, think of this. If dogs
and other predators cannot see color, why
would game need markings similar to their
surroundings to hide? If predators did not see
color, it would not matter.

Color consideration is important if you
are training a dog for field trials where an
orange tape marks the blind where the bird is
hidden. There should be no marker to signal
the handler; it also signals the dog.

Dogs have a wider field of vision then
humans. The size of the field of vision depends
upon the shape of the skull and placement of
the eyes. On the average, a dog can see for
about 250 degrees as compared to 180 degrees
for humans. The area a dog sees with both of
his or her eyes is referred to as his or her binocular vision. Binocular vision in a dog is much
less than for humans. The dog's range is about
one hundred degrees as compared to a human's

Amatuer Field Ch Kinnike B Seagate,
Owner: Charles Savage
              Photo courtesy of John Bandes

range of 140 degrees. Tests have suggested that dogs have poor depth perception and distance judgment. This is a very important fact to consider when teaching a dog to hunt. Poor depth perception and distance judgment can cause a dog to hesitate or be reluctant to do certain exercises. This is especially true for exercises that involve jumping into or over objects and from one object to another. These types of exercises must focus on building the dog's confidence and judgment.

Dogs see much better at night than humans do. This helps during night hunts and hunting in dark enclosed areas. Dogs do not see distant objects as well as humans, but they are much better at detecting movement. There is no research to suggest that the sight hound breeds have better vision than other breeds of dogs. Therefore, it is anyone's guess whether they see better or are just more visually tuned in.

Another sense of which people are not aware is the dog's sense of touch. Dogs have touch pads on their skin that are sensitive to pressure. A dog's hair is connected to sensory nerves that allow the dog to feel when its hair moves. This is one way a dog can feel his or her way around small places such as caves, tunnels, etc. This is one reason why dogs enjoy being petted as a reward for performing a command. Despite this sensitivity, dogs are not as aware of temperature differences as humans are.

One Handler

It is best if one person (other than a professional trainer) trains the dog. The main reason for this is each person is different and handles the dog differently. While a dog is learning, multiple handlers can confuse the dog. Once the dog knows what he or she has to do, he or she can deal with different handlers. However, when hunting, the dog and handler are a team and will work best when they work together. In the event that two people want to handle

Kinnike Lancaster at 6 months, Owner: Ronda Mansor
Photo courtesy of John Bandes

the same dog, all work should be duplicated to develop a dual handler/ dog team. Often a dog will do his or her job no matter who is behind him. Although the dog will work well, the handler may not feel confident working with the dog because he or she may not know how to read the dog.

Physical Warm-Up

While this is not a training technique, it is important for two reasons. First, if the dog finds the exercises physically uncomfortable, he or she will be less willing to do the work. If he or she is injured during training, he or she will be even less willing to go back into the same situation. Therefore, to prevent injury and discomfort, it is important to give the dog a chance to warm up before doing any work that requires any exercise beyond walking. It is a good idea to let the dog run on a flat, easy surface, fetching a ball or other object as a warm-up. This will also serve as an outlet for built up energy that usually results from the anticipation during the car ride to the training area. It will also allow the dog time to relieve himself. The length of the exercise will depend upon the weather and the dog's age and energy level. Be careful that the warm-up exercises do not make the dog too tired to work well.

3

Studying the Wind

In preparing for scent work, it is very helpful to understand just how the wind blows. The wind is ever changing, but you can get a "feel" for the different wind conditions. This is not as difficult to learn as you may think.

The first step is to start a journal. I like using a journal. No matter how much you think you will remember, you always forget something, and a journal retains the record. Each day that you go out to study the wind, enter the following information in your journal:

Date: _____**Day:**_____

Time: _____

Temperature and Humidity: It is important for you to learn the relationship between the time of day and the temperature.

Wind Direction: There are several ways to detect the direction of the wind. You can use flour or powder in a squirt bottle (such as the kind that mustard comes in) and send a puff of powder into the air. You can also use dust from the ground if the dust is dry. Toss some dust into the air to see which way it blows. You can use a piece of thread, weeds, or any other light object to see which way it blows. A cigarette lighter will also work well to show even the most gentle breeze.

If you are in the field, you can use a compass to decide which direction the wind is traveling. To do this, simply turn the base plate of the compass so that the printed arrow points to North (N). Next turn the compass until the red arrow or the needle of the compass aligns with the "N" on your compass. Notice which way the wind is blowing and make an imaginary line across the compass face, going in the direction of the wind. You will get a general idea of from which direction the wind is blowing and in which direction it is heading. While this will not be one hundred percent accurate, it is the best you can do in the field (Figure 3A).

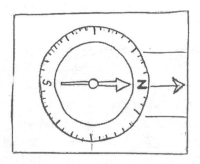

Figure 3A

Strength of the Wind: In a gentle breeze you can lightly feel the wind on your face or body. With the moderate breeze, grass and leaves will gently move. When the grass and leaves are bending gently, you have strong breeze conditions. If papers, leaves, and other light objects blow by, you have a very strong breeze.

Character of the Wind: Note if the wind is blowing steadily or shifting. If you use a smoke bomb or other visible means to check the wind, you can probably tell if the wind is looping, swirling, etc.

Terrain Features: It is important to make note of the terrain features because they will determine the direction and character of the wind. See the illustrations.

Once you have started a journal, you must study the wind in all different weather conditions. Gradually, you will develop a "feel" for what the wind does under different conditions. You will find that your ability to decide the relationship between the weather and wind is essential in mapping out your hunting strategy.

Ch Kinnike Hedda JH, Owner: Gene Heidenreich and Kinnike Kennels

Photo courtesy of John Bandes

After you have developed a "sense" about the wind, you are ready to study what scent does and how it moves in the wind. Keep in mind that scent, unlike wind, will cling to vegetation and leave a trail. Although wind just passes through, it carries the scent that leaves the trail. The movement of the wind will help you to learn where the scent trail is located.

Ch Kinnike True Colors JH, Owners: Jackie Savelli and Susan Tucker
   Photo by Susan Jonis, courtesy of John Bandes

4

Test the Wind

When training a dog for hunting, it is important always to know what the wind is doing, which way it is blowing. There are several ways to do this. You should use all of them at one time or another. One easy way to check the wind is to use a butane-style cigarette lighter. By lighting the lighter, you can watch the flame, which will respond to the slightest breeze, and detect which way it is blowing. Be sure when you test the wind that you always test it at your eye level as well as at the dog's nose level. In certain conditions and terrain, the wind will be different at each level.

Another method for testing the wind is to use a small smoke bomb. The smoke bomb is the most effective way to test how the wind is blowing from the game to the dog. To avoid contaminating the area with the odor of the smoke bomb, it is best to light the smoke bomb after the dog has found the game. You can then watch what the smoke does in relation to *where* the dog was working and *how* your dog was working. It will help you understand what scent was available to the dog.

Another technique is to use a small compressible object filled with powder. An example of this type of device is a mustard squeeze bottle. Another option is to tie sewing thread around your finger or wrist, allowing enough to hang down to see which way the wind is blowing.

5

The Nose

The dog's nose is a highly effective means of detecting scent. The nose is a chamber made of different cells. When the dog breathes normally, the air passes through the nose and does not hit the area that is most sensitive to scent, where the olfactory cells reside. These cells are at the top back part of the nose. When a dog breathes normally, the scent curves, the highest part of the curve hitting about the middle of the nose. Sniffing causes the air to eddy and hit the upper back part of the nose where the olfactory cells are found.

The dog's nose is also equipped to detect temperature and irritants. If irritants are

Timberline Bassett Hound Club Hunting Test, Fort Collins, Colorado

Photo courtesy of Carol Makowski

encountered, the nose will either secrete more fluid and/or the dog will sneeze. Keep in mind that irritants, for some dogs, can be pollen and the dust associated with a dry field.

Small hairs covered with mucus protrude from the olfactory cells. These hairs seem to be what detect the odors. Dogs have many more per cell than many other species. According to *Scent* by Milo D. Pearsall and Hugo Verbruggen, M.D., a cat has about forty hairs per cell. A man has six to eight hairs per cell, while the dog has one hundred to 150 hairs per cell. The number of olfactory cells in a dog is about 125 million while man has five million. Pearsall and Verbruggen explain the sensitivity of the dog's nose. "The dog can smell some odors at as much as one part per trillion (1 part per 1,000,000,000,000)...One of the substances released by human perspiration is butyric acid. If one gram of this chemical (a small drop in the bottom of a teaspoon) were to be spread throughout a ten-story building, a person could smell it at the window only at the moment of release. If this same amount were spread over the entire city of Philadelphia, a dog could smell it anywhere, even up to an altitude of 300 feet."

When you understand how the dog's nose physically functions, there is no doubt that other things affect his or her ability to detect scent. First the dog's health is important. The length and shape of the nose will enhance or hinder the dog's ability to detect scent. Thus, a dog such as a Boston terrier cannot detect scent as well as a collie. If a dog is taking

Timberline Bassett Hound Club Hunting Test, Fort Collins, Colorado

Photo courtesy of Carol Makowski

medications or if he or she has a dry nose, he or she may not be able to detect scent as well. Dryness can be caused by breathing dry air. Working in a dusty field will also hinder the dog's ability to detect scent. Some people call this "nose-fatigue." However, it is different from the "nose-fatigue" that humans experience.

When a human works in an area where a smell is constant, such as a flower shop, after awhile the person will not smell the flowers. The dog does not seem to react in the same way. This has been proven by dogs who continue to follow the same scent over a period of time. Their ability to detect the scent is not affected by boredom or fatigue. In an article in *Dog Fancy Magazine* titled, "The Canine Olfactory System is the Dog's Most Amazing Attribute," W. Bradford Swift states, "One Bloodhound on record followed a human scent for 114 miles." A larger part of the dog's brain is dedicated to the sense of smell than in a human's. With more of his or her brain devoted to the sense of smell, a dog is better able to tell what and how much he or she smells than a human can. This is just one reason why it is never a good idea to try to tell your dog what he or she smells or where the scent is located. If your dog is trained and is healthy, you must learn to trust your dog, even when you think he or she is wrong.

Arthur Ward Lindsey, Ph.D. Sc.D, explains in the book *American Sporting Dogs* that scent is more meaningful to a dog than sight. He gives the following example. "I once accompanied a new acquaintance to his home and as we entered the yard was inspected by a fine Airedale and accepted as his master's friend. Almost two years later, I went back to that house alone. The Airedale stiffened and growled. I spoke to him or her, and he came down the walk, sniffed me, and promptly wagged what was left of his tail! Vision had not recorded me as a friend, but scent did so at once."

Ch Kinnike Mickey of True Colors JH
Photo courtesy of John Bandes

6

Scent

What Is It?

When training a hunting dog, it helps to understand what scent is and how it behaves. Scent is made of many different things. It is left on the ground by various elements of the animal's body. Animals give off skin cells that collect on the ground. They also lose hair that has skin cells on it and body oils. All other liquids that come from the animal will leave scent. This would include mucus, saliva, sweat, scent glad secretions, and "tears." Scent is also left by the gases that come from an animal. These gases come from the lungs and digestive tract. The scent of an animal changes with its state of health. The types of food an animal eats will also affect the scent it gives off. The mental condition of the animal causes the chemistry to change and will also change the scent. This does not mean that a rabbit will smell like a bird, but subtle changes in the intensity will occur. There will also be a difference between male and female scent. Each time the animal eliminates waste products, it leaves very strong scent that lingers, even after the solid waste has dissolved into the ground.

Timberline Bassett Hound Club Hunting Test, Fort Collins, Colorado

Photo courtesy of Carol Makowski

Once the scent-causing substances hit the ground, the environment will change them. This means that both weather and time will alter the scent once it leaves the animal's body. Never forget that scent is the result of the chemical properties of the source. Therefore, consider Dr. Lindsey's statement in *American Sporting Dogs*. "A more elusive variable is the effect of physical conditions on the intensity of a scent...Molecular activity, which is the basis of volatility, increases generally with temperature; hence low temperatures cannot be expected to favor the detection of scents. Humidity must also have an effect, but here the results are less likely to be uniform. A heavy dew, by dissolving the minute traces of mineral on a trail, may render some more volatile and hence may improve the scent, but enough water may also wash away and disperse their traces and so obliterate the trail."

Lindsey goes on to explain that the dog that enters the field will be assaulted with a variety of animal scents. Many of these scents may be stronger than the scent of the particular species of animal you wish the dog to find. Lindsey explains that training, not instinct, is the reason why a dog will not chase the "hot" scent of the rabbit but will stay with the faint scent of the bird. He illustrates training versus instinct with this example. There is "probably no greater proof of this relationship than the apparent offensiveness of the scent of woodcocks to bird dogs. Evidently these birds are actually repugnant to them, yet a well-trained dog will hunt and retrieve woodcocks when his master sets him at the task." Keep in mind that scent is not the only variable that makes a good bird dog. "Variability in the field performance of dogs may result from differences in any of these associated factors. Even in the same breed, dogs may have good noses or poor…The performance of dogs is much more likely to vary through the clash of their inherent interest in the scents that they pick up and the attention that they have been trained to give them to serve their masters' wishes. Even a good bird dog can be diverted by the scent of a rabbit unless he or she has learned that unpleasant results come from chasing rabbits."

Dr. Lindsey mentions that hunters claim that game can withhold its scent. "In support, hunters cite the failure of dogs to pick up a scent even when the quarry has actually been sighted." As Dr. Lindsey points out in his book, it is impossible for an animal to withhold its scent. He explains that an animal that is very quiet, tired, or immobile will not give off as much scent as one that is active and rested. This fact coupled with the weather conditions may cause a dog to miss the trace elements of scent that are available.

There are also factors about scent that we do not understand. Dr. Lindsey says that "Mr. G. B. Hunter of Newark, Ohio, who is more interested in his dogs than in shooting and as a result is a keen student of dog behavior, reports that during the breeding season when quail have chicks, a dog fails to pick up their scent even where the birds are abundant." Could this be a survival mechanism? Perhaps we will never know.

Learning how scent behaves will help to solve many problems that the hunter encounters in the field. It may help to answer some questions about why a dog misses a scent or why a dog works better one day than another.

How Scent Behaves

Always keep in mind that the closer a dog gets to the game, the stronger the scent becomes. This is because the scent is "fresher" and more concentrated. This is probably why the bird dog that sets or points can stop at the correct distance from the bird without flushing it. Of course, it takes practice for the dog to learn just how close he or she can get. There is no way for us to tell if the dog's keen sense of hearing comes into play in this situation or not. At some point, the dog will hear the bird running, breathing, or making other noises.

It is easier to figure out what causes scent than it is to decide how scent behaves. It is true that we will never know exactly what a dog does or does not detect when following scent. Yet we can help our hunting dog find the scent that is available if we understand how scent behaves. To do this, you must know about wind, weather, and terrain. These three elements influence how much scent is available and where the scent travels. (See the chapter "Studying the Wind.")

Depending upon the weather conditions, the scent that an animal gives off forms a scent cone. The animal is the point of the cone. As the scent leaves the animal, it spreads wider and wider to form the base of the cone. The further the scent travels from the animal, the wider the scent cone becomes. It is the job of the hunting dog to look for the cone and follow it to its source. Notice in Figure 6A that the scent can form a cone as it travels along the ground or as it rises into the air.

Figure 6A

In many respects, scent will behave in the same manner as liquids and smoke. Scent will flow down a slope following the path of least resistance. Therefore, you are more likely to find scent in a gully or drainage path such as the ones etched into the landscape by heavy rain (Figure 6B).

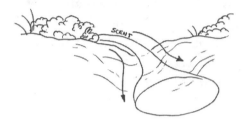

Figure 6B

Scent will rise from its source, reach a high spot in the air, and loop back down to the ground. In each place where the scent returns to the ground, it collects in the spot where it touches the ground. When scent loops, it can loop several times leaving many pools of scent with no obvious trail or line leading to the game. The dog will come along, hit the spot, and not be able to follow the scent to its source (Figure 6C). If the source of the scent is in a depression, such as a small valley, the scent can travel up the slopes nearby. In these conditions, the scent acts in the same manner as smoke going up a chimney. This is usually caused by the rise of warm air during the day, which carries the scent with it (Figure 6D).

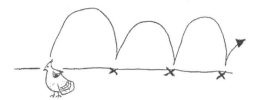

Figure 6C

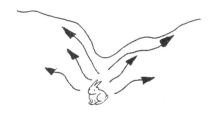

Figure 6D

The reverse can happen as the air cools and falls to the low areas. Scent can be carried down a drainage gully or any other terrain feature that would channel the scent. When this happens, the scent will pool in the low area (Figure 6E).

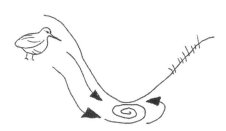

Figure 6E

Terrain features such as tree lines, rock walls, and plowed fields influence where scent travels. These obstacles can cause scent to eddy, swirl around trees, move behind a wall, and travel over a wall, leaking scent into a clearing (Figure 6F). On dry, hot days with no noticeable breeze, the scent can rise straight up. In these situations, the dog will not find the animal or bird unless he or she walks right over it.

In rough terrain and in gusty shifting winds, the scent can travel in many directions. It can collect in nooks and crannies in the same manner as debris does that has been washed down a river. Scent clings to objects such as walls, brush, or low areas (Figure 6G and Figure 6H).

Figure 6F

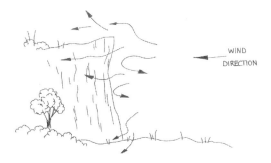

Figure 6G

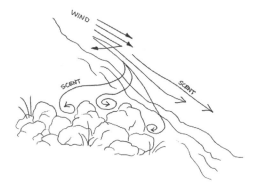

Figure 6H

Animals or birds hidden in dense vegetation, especially vegetation with low broad leaves, cause another problem. It is likely that the scent will become trapped with little or no leakage (Figure 6I).

Figure 6I

Humidity increases the availability of scent for a dog. Scent that "dries out" during the day may "revive" in the damp of the evening or in the morning or after light rain. The dampness will release what has soaked into the ground. However, a downpour will wash the scent away. Usually the early morning, evening, and night are the best times for the dog to pick up scent. During the day is the poorest time for the dog to work. In the morning as the ground warms, the scent cone will rise. Scent from warm birds and animals or warm areas will rise in cool or cold air. In situations where the scent is most likely to rise, it is best to work your dog above low areas. This will allow your dog to detect the scent that is rising (Figure 6J).

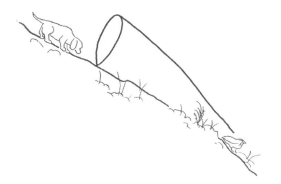

Figure 6J

In the evening, the opposite takes place. The scent travels down or will rise a little and then return to the ground. This is the best time to use a dog since the most scent will be available at ground level. It is also best to work your dog in the low areas to catch the scent from the birds or animals above you (Figure 6K and 3L).

Figure 6K

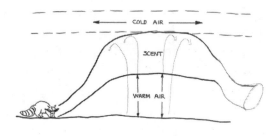

Figure 6L

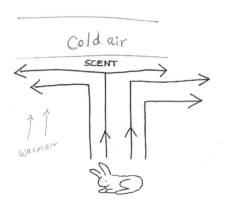

Figure 6M

If there is a cold layer of air above with warm air beneath, the scent will rise and hang around. This is the same condition that produces smog alerts and causes smoke to hang in the air. If a dog is working on flat ground, he or she may have difficulty detecting the scent. This is because the scent will hang around higher up and not be available at ground level (Figure 6M). If your dog detects scent on a hill or mountain and loses it above and below the scent band, you can check different parts of the hill and mountain to try to locate the source of the scent. When your dog has several "hits," the combination of hits can point the direction to the source of the scent. If a bird or animal is hidden long enough and scent pooling takes place (little or no breeze to move the scent around), the scent pool can saturate the area making it difficult for the dog to locate the source of the scent (Figure 6N).

Figure 6N

Sometimes, there will not be much of a scent pool for the dog to detect, causing the dog to miss it entirely. When a bird or animal is very still, it will give off much less scent than when it is moving. A moving animal or bird raises its body heat, which helps to generate more scent. The amount of scent that is available is dictated by the amount of exposed body. For example, an animal that has "gone to ground" will give off a very small scent pool. The scent available in the "gone to ground" situation is the residual scent left by the animal as it ran into the den or hole. The scent does not rise very much from out of the den, although it will collect in the den. This is why a dog can run past a den in the ground and not find it. Yet once the dog finds the hole, she will get very excited and stick her nose in the hole, often snorting as she inhales the scent from the animal.

As scent travels over an area, the terrain features can cause "dead" spaces to form where no scent has been carried. Generally, these dead spaces are in tucked away areas where the wind has blown past the space but not into the space. The scent from animals hiding in these "dead" spaces can be trapped or blocked by the passing breeze. An example of a dead area would be the base of a sheer cliff. Wind blowing off the top of the cliff and angling down can miss the base of the cliff (Figure 6O).

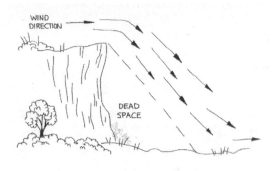

Figure 6O

Another combination that could cause a dead space is a depression and a strong breeze. The strong breeze would blow the scent over the depression instead of into it. If your dog is following a scent and loses it, this could be the result of a dead space. Generally, you should move on to try to pick up the scent again (Figure 6P).

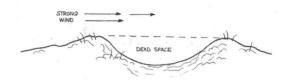

Figure 6P

The way scent travels and its availability depend upon the following elements: weather, terrain, age of the scent trail and source, the condition of the scent source, the air flow, wind, vegetation, concealment of the source, and the time of day you are hunting. The combination of these factors makes each situation unique. It is up to you to analyze the conditions in each situation so that you can learn how your dog reacts in these various conditions. By doing so you can decide what your dog is telling you. With this information, you can direct your dog in a way that will lead the dog to the game. You and your dog are a team, each with his or her specific job and area of expertise.

7

Grid Patterns

An essential element in hunting is knowing how to use the wind to your advantage. The methods for using the wind are the same no matter what type of game you are hunting. As any avid hunter knows, the animal he or she hunts uses the wind to its advantage to avoid the hunter. Therefore, if the hunter wants to find the game, he or she must allow his or her dog to use the wind to the dog's advantage. This can become a contest between the dog and the game.

Your correct assessment of the wind and weather, along with a practical grid pattern, is not only important for hunting, it is important for training. If the dog is allowed to succeed with a good combination of wind and grid patterns, the dog will learn how to use the wind to his or her favor. During search and rescue missions and training sessions, I have watched experienced dogs work the wind like an expert. I have also seen the inexperienced dogs waste time and effort until they "fine tune" their techniques. After awhile, a SAR dog will only need to be told what type of mission he or she is on, not what to do. The same is true for a good hunting dog. As dogs gain experience, they learn to slow down, assess the area, and figure out just where to look for game.

Working the wind to your advantage is not very difficult. As a rule of thumb, a dog handler will work his or her dog perpendicular to the direction of the wind. This will give the dog the best advantage to pick up an available scent cone. With the dog going upwind (the dog facing into the wind) you can track the dog's hits and learn from which direction the scent is coming. With a steady breeze, working your dog down wind, you can detect the source of the scent. However, in variable wind conditions and rough terrain, the source of the scent can be difficult to detect. In a variable wind situation, you can double grid an area, which will require you to reduce the size of your hunting area.

As you grid an area, your dog will range or quarter within a prescribed distance. While you are walking your grid pattern, your dog should quarter back and forth in front of or around you. Some dogs weave back and forth (Figure 7A), and some dogs circle you (Figure 7B). The size of the area that the dog quarters or ranges is taught to the dog. Although the dog's personality and breed will influence his or her ranging area, you must teach the dog how far to go or how close to stay to you.

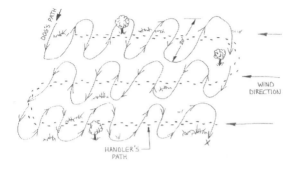

Figure 7A

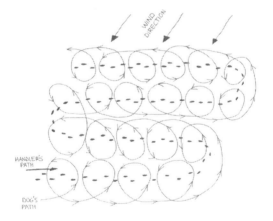

Figure 7B

If you have a steady wind coming from any direction, you should work your dog perpendicular to the wind (Figure 7C). The handler should try to walk his or her dog so that the dog crosses the wind.

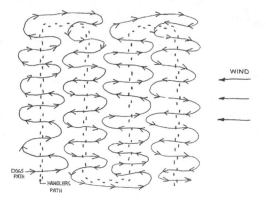

Figure 7C

There are some things you can do when you are in a situation where your dog quarters far and/or in situations where the terrain forces you to work into the wind. You can get your dog to work across the wind while you walk into the wind by directing the dog's quartering or ranging pattern to cross the wind (Figure 7D).

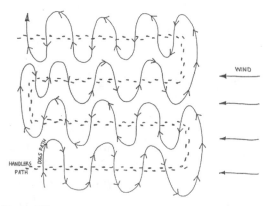

Figure 7D

If the wind is shifting, you may have to combine the grid patterns in Figures 4C and 4D. Sometimes due to terrain and wind, you may have to work around impassable objects. If this happens, you should try to get back on track when you can and complete your grid pattern. Remember, it is the dog's job to search the areas you cannot reach yourself (Figure 7E).

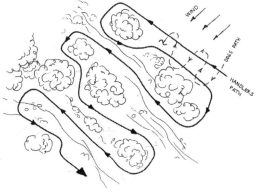

Figure 7E

8

The Training Log

Just as you kept a journal to learn how to study the wind, you should keep a training log when you work with your dog. Your training log should include all of the information you had in your wind journal and a few more categories as well.

Date, Day
Time
Temperature
Humidity
Wind Direction
Strength of Wind
Character of Wind
Terrain Features

Training Area: This should include a description of your training area such as the brush cover, obstacles, bodies of water, etc.

Type of Problem: You want to describe just how you set up the problem for your dog: what you did, what you used, how you placed your scent source, etc.

How You Worked the Dog: Explain how you worked your dog. Include what you did, how you gridded the area, changed direction, redirected your dog, etc.

How Your Dog Worked: You want to detail how your dog worked in relationship to the problems at hand. Did the dog run right in to the scent source? Did the dog circle the area and not locate the scent source? How did you decide where the scent was found? One way to do this would be to set off a smoke bomb after the problem is over. While it is fresh in your mind, you can record why you think the dog did what he or she did.

What You Can Do to Help the Dog Work Better: Again, while it is fresh in your mind, you can write down how you could set up another problem to teach your dog to do what you want. You can also record what you can do to correct a problem.

It may seem like a chore to keep a training log. However, in terms of looking back on your training sessions, even years later, you will find that a log will jog your memory. It will allow you to recall details about your successes and failures. This helps if you discuss training techniques with other hunters. It also allows you to exactly reproduce later a training method you used years ago with a similar dog. A training log also tracks your success rate with your dog. If you feel that your dog has hit a low spot, you can look back at the log and find out whether it happened before. You can also see just how much progress you have made and how quickly you have done it.

9

Training With Grid Patterns and Reading Your Dog

Training a dog with grid patterns is easy to do. Using a grid pattern will also give the dog the experience necessary to hunt successfully. The first step is to check the wind. The second step is to place your scent source or article at a distance that is fair for your dog to work. This distance should be based on his or her age and level of training. The article should be placed UPWIND (Figure 9A). Following the grid pattern in Figures 7C or 7D, work your dog until he or she finds the object. If the dog is green, the distance between the starting point and the article should be short. You should also start training in an easy area that is flat and free of obstacles.

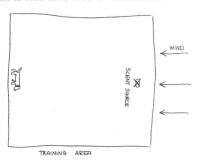

Figure 9A

As your dog gets better, increase the size of the area, and add the types of terrain features through which the dog must learn to hunt.

If your dog gets the scent of the object, he or she will abandon the grid pattern and work the scent cone. As he or she does this, his or her quartering or ranging pattern will decrease until he or she finds the scent source (Figure 9B).

Figure 9B

If the scent is looping, the dog will hit on scent pools, but not be able to find the source of the scent. If this happens, you must note the pattern of the hits. Guide the dog in the direction you feel the scent is coming from based on the weather and wind (Figure 9C). Sometimes you may have to continue your grid pattern even if the dog has trouble. The dog may pass the scent source unless he or she walks on top of it. This is an important lesson for the dog. When scent loops, it usually does not form a very large scent pool on the ground where the animal is hidden. Never forget that the total body mass of the quarry is not big to begin with.

If the wind is swirling and changing, you should grid your area using the patterns in Figures 9C and 9D to be sure to cover the entire area.

Figure 9C

The way you place the scent source in training exercises is important. All hunting dogs will both air scent and track, depending upon where the scent is strongest. Most of the time, the hound will work with his or her nose to the ground. It is also not unusual to see the hound raise his or her nose and test the air at his or her head level when he or she gets a whiff of airborne scent. You should go to great pains to place your scent source so that you meet the following conditions.

First, the scent source must not always be directly in front of the dog. For example, if a dog learns that a trail always goes straight away from him or her, he or she will never look for it elsewhere. Therefore, a dog must learn to follow a trail or airborne scent that comes from every direction (Figure 9D).

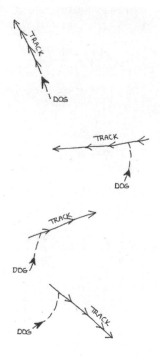

Figure 9D

Second, you must be certain that your own scent does not act as a beacon to the dog to lead him or her to the animal scent source. You may have to arrange for someone else to drop the animal scent off upwind from your training area. This will set up your problem so that there is NO human scent trail in your training area (Figure 9E). If you are working with a scent drag, you may have to get other people to drag the scent source.

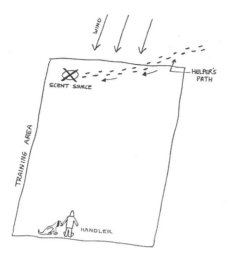

Figure 9E

Third, in the beginning of training, you need to know where the scent source is located so that you can watch your dog and see how he or she reacts as he or she gets closer to the scent source. This is the way you learn how to read your dog. After awhile you can probably tell how "hot" the scent is by the way the dog works. However, the real test of your dog's skills is to find a scent source when *you* do not know where the game is hidden. All people—no matter whether they are aware of it or not—give some signal to their dog when the dog gets close to the scent source. Some dogs are observant enough to detect the signal. Therefore, if your dog can find game when you do not know where it is, you can be sure that the dog is not following a subconscious signal that you are giving him. This is the real test of your handling skills and your dog's hunting skills. If you are working with blinds, have someone place a bird in the blind for you. Let the human scent cool down for fifteen to twenty minutes or more. Next, send your dog to find the bird. This is a great test in a field where there is high grass or brush and the game could be anywhere.

10

The Rewards

The sport of hunting has been around for centuries. There is nothing quite like working with a dog on a crisp autumn day. Each breed of hunting dog is a work of art when doing what it was bred to do. Each hunter has his or her own reasons for choosing a particular breed and the type of game that he or she likes to hunt. No matter what the type of game, all hunters share the joy of the hunt. The excitement the dog feels matches none other. The dogs live for the days in the field and get a look of satisfaction at the end of the day that only a hunter can appreciate.

When we watch our dogs sleep, see their paws twitch, hear their sleep-veiled yips and their thumping tails, it is easy to imagine that, in their dreams, they are on a blissful hunt.

Hunting with a dog provides a bond between dog and man that goes back to the beginning of the dog-man relationship. You get a special feeling when you work as a team with your dog. Both of you must do your part to have a successful hunt.

Field trials add a special edge to the hunt, sparked by the competition between contestants. The dogs seem to pick up on that as well and sometimes give a bit extra to the effort.

It does not matter whether you hunt the field or trial your dog. The joy of the activity, the teamwork between dog and human, and the bond created are unbeatable.

Ch Kinnike Hillary JH
Photo courtesy of John Bandes

Appendix I

To obtain "Click and Treat" material contact:

Direct Book Service
    PO Box 2778
    701B Poplar
    Wenatchee, WA 98807-2778
    1-800-776-2665
    FAX 1-509-663-9115

Sunshine Books Inc.
    49 River Street, Suite 3
    Waltham, MA 02453-8345
    1-800-472-5425

For sheepherding whistles contact:

Border Collies In Action
    Rt 2 Box 540
    Tulelake, CA 96134
    1-800-833-0332
    Email: bcollie@cdsnet.net
    Websitet: www.cdsnet.net/business/BCollie

Border Corner
    PO Box 340
    Biggs, CA 95917
    1-916-846-2020
    FAX 1-916-846-5815

Appendix II lists many of the sporting dogs throughout the world. For further reference, you can consult
the following sources:

The ATLAS of Dog Breeds of the World, by Bonnie
  Wilcox, DVM, and Chris Walkowicz, Published by t.f.h.

Simon & Schuster's Guide to Dogs, published by
  Simon & Schuster

The Great Book of Dogs, by Gino Pugnetti, published by Galahad Books

A Celebration of Rare Breeds, by Cathy J.
  Flamholtz, published by OTR Publications

Appendix II

The Hounds

French Hounds

Griffon Nivernais
Grand Griffon Vendeen
Briquet Griffon Vendeen
Grand Basset Griffon Vendeen
Petit Basset Griffon Vendeen
Grand Bleu de Gascogne
Petit Griffon Bleu de Gascogne
Basset Bleu de Gascogne
Poitevin
Grand Gascon Saintongeois
Petit Gascon Saintongeois
Griffon Fauve de Bretagne
Basset Fauve de Bretagne
Chin d'Artois
Basset Artesien Normand
Billy
Levesque
Ariegeois
Porcelaine
Beagle Harrier
Chien Francais Blanc et Noir
Chien Francais Flanc et Orange
Chien Francais Tricolore
Grand Anglo-Francais
Moyen Anglo-Francais
Petit Anglo-Francais

Spain

Sabueso Espanol de Monte
Sabueso Espanol Lebrero

Italy

Segugio Italiano a Pelo Raso
Segugio Italiano a Pelo Forte

Yugoslavia

Wirehaired Istrain Hound
Smoothhaired Istrian Hound
Posavac Hound
Bosnian Roughhaired Hound
Balkan Hound
Yugoslavian Mountain Hound
Yugoslavian Tricolored Hound

Greece

Greek Harehound

Hungary

Tall Transylvanian Hound
Short Transylvanian Hound

Czechoslovakia

Black Forest Hound

Poland

Polish Hound

Germany

Deutsche Bracke
Westphalian Dachsbracke
Hanoverian Schweisshund
Bavarian Mountain Hound
Standard Dachshund
Miniature Dachshund
Steinbracke

Belgium

Bloodhound

Austria

Austrian Brandlebracke
Styrian Roughhaired Mountain Hound
Tyroler Bracke
Alpine Dachsbracke

Switzerland

Schweizer Laufhund
Schweizer Niederlaufhund
Bruno Jura Laufhund
St. Hubert Jura Laufhund
Jura Niederlaufhund
Berner Laufhund
Berner Niederlaufhund
Luzerner Laufhund
Luzerner Niederlaufhund

Denmark

Strellufstover

Finland

Finnish Hound

Sweden

Jamthund
Drever
Schillerstovar
Hamiltonstovare
Smalandsstovare

Norway

Haldenstovare
Hygenhund
Dunker
Norwegian Elkhound

Great Britain

English Foxhound
Beagle
Harrier
Basset Hound
Otter Hound
Hanover Hound
Basenji
Ireland
Kerry Beagle

USA

Trigg Hound
American Foxhound
American Black and Tan Coonhound
Redbone Coonhound
English Coonhound
Bluetick Coonhound
Redtick Coonhound
Treeing Walker Coonhound
American Blue Gascon Hound
Majestic Tree Hound
Plott Hound
Leopard Cur
Mountain Cur
Treeing Tennessee Brindle
Stephens Stock
Black Mouth Cur

USSR

Russian Hound
Russian Harlequin Hound
Estonian Hound
Latvian Hound
Lithuanian Hound
Karelian Bear Dog

The Gun Dogs

Water Dogs

France

Barber
Standard Poodle

Ireland

Irish Water Spaniel

Great Britian

Curly-Coated Retriever

Netherlands

Wetterhoun

USA

American Water Spaniel

Portugal

Portuguese Water Dog

Pointers

Belguim

Belgian Shorthaired Pointer

France

Wirehaired Pointing Griffon
Braque d'Auvergne
Braque d'Ariege
Braque du Bourbonnais
Braque Dupuy
Braque Francais de Grande Taille
Braque Francais de Petite Taille
Braque Saint-Germain

Great Britian

> Pointer

Denmark

> Old Danish Bird Dog
> Hertha Pointer

Czechosloviakia

> Cesky Fousek

Hungary

> Vizsla

Italy

> Bracco Italiano
> Spinone Italiano

Spain

> Perdiguero de Burgos
> Perdiguero Navarro

Portugal

> Perdigueriro

Germany

> German Shorthaired Pointer
> German Wirehaired Pointer
> Stichelhaar
> Weimaraner
> Pudelpointer
> Wachtelhund (German Spaniel)

Retrievers

Great Britian

> Flat-Coated Retriever
> Labrador Retriever
> Golden Retriever

Canada

    Nova Scotia Duck Tolling Retriever

Netherlands

    Kooikerhondje

USA

    Chesapeake Bay Retriever

Setters

Germany

    German Longhaired Pointer
    Large Munsterlander
    Small Munsterlander

Great Britian

    English Setter
    Gordon Setter

Ireland

    Irish Setter
    Irish Red and White Setter

Netherlands

    Stabyhoun
    Drentse Patrijshond

France

    Brittany
    Epagneul Francais
    Epagneul Picard
    Epagneul Blue de Picardie
    Epagneul Pont-Audemer

Germany

    Deutscher Wachtelhund

Flushing Spaniels

Great Britain

Sussex Spaniel
Field Spaniel
English Cocker Spaniel
English Springer Spaniel
Welsh Springer Spaniel
Clumber Spaniel

USSR

Russian Spaniel

USA

American Cocker Spaniel
Boykin Spaniel

Index